Piano Exam Pieces

ABRSM Grade 5

Selected from the 2015 & 2016 syllabus

Name

Date

GW00497363

Contents

Editor for ABRSM: Richard Jones

page

LIST A

1   **Johann Sebastian Bach** Prelude in C minor: No. 2 from *Six Préludes für Anfänger auf dem*   2
Clavier, BWV 934

2   **Jan Ladislav Dussek** Allegro non tanto: first movement from Sonatina in G, Op. 19 No. 1   4

3   **Ignace Joseph Pleyel** Adagio: second movement from Sonata in B flat, B. 571   6

LIST B

1   **Johann Friedrich Franz Burgmüller** L'orage: No. 13 from *Études de genre*, Op. 109   9

2   **Reyngol'd Moritsevich Glier** Gaiamente: No. 3 from *12 esquisses*, Op. 47   12

3   **Heinrich Hofmann** Am Abend: No. 2 from *Stimmungsbilder*, Op. 88   14

LIST C

1   **Béla Bartók** Este a székelyeknél: No. 5 from *10 könnyű zongoradarab*   17

2   **Alexandre Tansman** Cache-cache: No. 4 from *Pour les enfants*, Vol. 4   20

3   **Evelien Vis** 60s Swing: No. 1 from *Swinging Rhythms*   22

Other pieces for Grade 5

LIST A

4   **Handel** Entrée in G minor (from HWV 453). No. 10 from Handel, *Easy Piano Pieces and Dances* (Bärenreiter)

5   **Haydn** Minuet in C minor. *The Classical Spirit*, Book 1 (Alfred)

6   **Mozart** Allegro: 1st movt from 'Viennese' Sonatina No. 6 in C. Mozart, *Six Viennese Sonatinas* (Schott)

LIST B

4   **Bridge** Allegretto con moto: No. 1 from *Miniature Pastorals*, 1st Set (Boosey & Hawkes). Also available in:
Bridge, *Nine Miniature Pastorals* (Thames)

5   **Jensen** Lied, Op. 33 No. 10. *More Romantic Pieces for Piano*, Book 3 (ABRSM)

6   **Maikapar** Prelude in F: No. 19 from *20 Preludes for Pedal*, Op. 38 (Prhythm)

LIST C

4   **Valerie Capers** Sweet Mister Jelly Roll: No. 3 from *Portraits in Jazz* (OUP)

5   **Shande Ding** To the Suburbs: 1st movt from *Suite for Children. Chinese Piano Music for Children* (Schott)

6   **Shostakovich** Dance: No. 7 from *Dances of the Dolls* (Boosey & Hawkes)

First published in 2014 by ABRSM (Publishing) Ltd,
a wholly owned subsidiary of ABRSM, 24 Portland
Place, London W1B 1LU, United Kingdom
© 2014 by The Associated Board of the Royal
Schools of Music

Music origination by Julia Bovee
Cover by Kate Benjamin & Andy Potts
Printed in England by Headley Brothers
Ltd, The Invicta Press, Ashford, Kent.

A:1

Prelude in C minor

No. 2 from *Six Préludes für Anfänger auf dem Clavier*, BWV 934

J. S. Bach
(1685–1750)

Six Préludes für Anfänger auf dem Clavier Six Preludes for Beginners at the Keyboard

Essential to Bach's teaching methods were the preludes he wrote to act as composition models and keyboard studies for his pupils. His first biographer, J. N. Forkel, wrote that: 'If [Bach] found that anyone, after some months of practice, began to lose patience, he was kind enough to write little connected pieces in which their exercises were combined together. Of this kind are the *Six Préludes für Anfänger auf dem Clavier…* He wrote them down during the hours of teaching and, in doing so, attended only to the momentary need of the student. But afterwards he transformed them into beautiful, expressive little works of art.'

The second of the set, selected here, has the ¾ time and flowing quavers of the Italian corrente, though the very same broken-chordal figuration as in bb. 5–8 occurs in some of Bach's minuets. Dynamics are left to the player's discretion. The ornaments in bb. 2 and 4 may be reduced to an acciaccatura only, played on the beat. Either version would be acceptable in the exam.

Source: MS copies, Berlin, Staatsbibliothek Preussischer Kulturbesitz, Musikabteilung, Mus.ms.Bach P528, P540, P542, P672, P885

© 1988 by The Associated Board of the Royal Schools of Music
Adapted from J. S. Bach et al.: *A Little Keyboard Book*, edited by Richard Jones (ABRSM)

A:2

Allegro non tanto

First movement from Sonatina in G, Op. 19 No. 1

J. L. Dussek
(1760–1812)

Jan Ladislav Dussek was a Bohemian composer and keyboard virtuoso who established an international career: he was active at various times in Germany, France, England, the Netherlands, Russia and Lithuania, as well as in his native Bohemia. During his London period (1789–99) he became a fashionable piano teacher, set up a music publishing business with his father-in-law, and performed on several occasions with Haydn, who commented on his 'remarkable talents'.

The six sonatinas of Op. 19 were originally published in a version 'avec accompagnement d'une flûte', but they were soon reissued for solo keyboard. In the movement selected here, after the forthright opening theme, marked *forte*, the texture of the subsidiary theme at b. 5 invites a lighter touch and a reduced dynamic. On its first statement, this subsidiary theme ends with a *forte* G in b. 9, introducing a reprise of the original theme. On its second statement, the subsidiary theme ends on G sharp in b. 17 – a dramatic moment that suggests varied dynamics (note the composer's *p* and *pp* in bb. 22 and 23) till the concluding reprise of the main theme at b. 25.

Source: *Six Sonatines pour le fortepiano ou le clavecin*, Op. 19 (London: Longman & Broderip, *c*.1792)

© 2014 by The Associated Board of the Royal Schools of Music

A:3

Adagio

Second movement from Sonata in B flat, B. 571

I. J. Pleyel
(1757–1831)

The Austrian composer Ignace Joseph Pleyel studied and lodged with Haydn from around 1772. He became assistant to the Kapellmeister at Strasbourg Cathedral in about 1784, rising to the position of Kapellmeister in 1789. During the years 1791–2 he conducted the so-called Professional Concerts in London, where he renewed his friendship with Haydn. In 1795 he settled in Paris, opening a music shop and founding a publishing house, known as the Maison Pleyel. He also established a piano-making firm in the French capital in 1807.

In the late 18th century, there was a huge public demand for Pleyel's music, and by 1800 he had become one of the most successful composers in Europe. His Classical style, in many ways akin to that of Haydn and Mozart, is well illustrated by this Adagio from his Sonata in B flat, which was also issued 'for piano and violin ad lib.'. Dynamics are left to the player's discretion.

Source: *Deux grandes sonates*, Op. 7 (London: Longman & Broderip, 1787)

da Capo [al Fine]

L'orage

No. 13 from *Études de genre*, Op. 109

B:1

J. F. F. Burgmüller
(1806–74)

L'orage The Storm; **Études de genre** Characteristic Studies

Johann Friedrich Franz Burgmüller, German by birth, settled in Paris after 1832. There he became very popular as a pianist and composer, improvising hundreds of salon pieces and composing much piano music for teaching purposes. Many of his short piano pieces have programmatic titles.

The 18 pieces of Burgmüller's *Études de genre*, Op. 109, were first published in 1858. No. 13, 'L'orage', gives a vivid evocation of a storm, with its unsettled dynamics, *sforzandi*, rumbling effects (bb. 2 and 4, etc.) and sudden thunderclap (b. 14). Peace is restored at the change to the tonic major D (b. 20), though even here the rumbling of distant thunder is heard in the bass.

Source: *18 Characteristic Studies (Études de genre)*, Op. 109 (London: Augener, 1903)

© 1986 by the Associated Board of the Royal Schools of Music
Adapted from *Short Romantic Pieces for Piano*, Book III, edited by Lionel Salter (ABRSM)

Un poco più lento

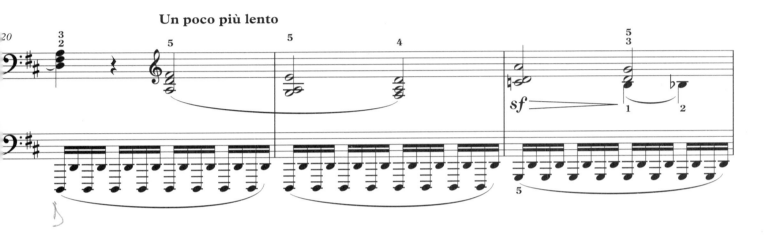

rit. **a tempo**

rall.

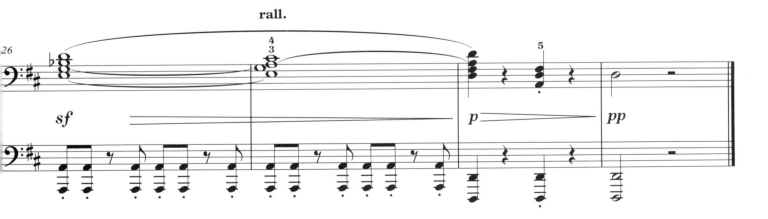

B:2

Gaiamente

No. 3 from *12 esquisses*, Op. 47

Edited by Thomas A. Johnson

R. M. Glier
(1875–1956)

Gaiamente Gaily, merrily; **Esquisses** Sketches

The Russian composer Reyngol'd Moritsevich Glier studied at the Moscow Conservatory, where he became professor of composition in 1920. Earlier, in 1902–4, he had served as tutor to Prokofiev. His compositions are a late offshoot of the Russian Romantic tradition of the 19th century. He is best-known for his large-scale works – operas, symphonies, concertos and ballets.

   Glier's *12 esquisses*, Op. 47, was first published in 1910. No. 3, selected here, derives its distinctive character from its quintuple ($\frac{5}{4}$) metre. Each bar is, in effect, subdivided into two plus three crotchets (excepting only the link bar 26), as in the similarly $\frac{5}{4}$ second movement from Tchaikovsky's *Symphonie pathétique*. Both pieces are somewhat scherzo-like and yet highly lyrical in a recognizably Russian manner, and it is not impossible that the Tchaikovsky movement served as Glier's model.

Source: *Douze esquisses pour piano*, Op. 47 (Moscow and Leipzig: Jürgenson, 1910)

B:3

Am Abend

No. 2 from *Stimmungsbilder*, Op. 88

Heinrich Hofmann
(1842–1902)

Am Abend In the Evening; **Stimmungsbilder** Mood Pictures

The German composer and pianist Heinrich Hofmann became a chorister at Berlin Cathedral at the age of nine. In 1857, aged 15, he enrolled as a student at Kullak's music school in the same city, the Neue Akademie der Tonkunst. Later he established himself as a concert pianist, a music teacher and a prolific composer – his music became very popular in Germany in the 1870s and 1880s. He is known today mainly for his short piano pieces, many of which have programmatic titles.

Hofmann's *Stimmungsbilder*, Op. 88, which is subtitled *Kleine Vortragsstücke in leichter Spielart* (little performing pieces in a simple playing style), was first published in 1887. The second piece in the collection, 'Am Abend', rather than painting a picture in sound, evokes a dreamy, romantic atmosphere often associated with the evening.

Source: *Stimmungsbilder*, Op. 88 (Hannover: Steingräber, 1887)

Adapted from H. Hofmann: *17 Miscellaneous Pieces*, edited by Thomas A. Johnson (ABRSM)

Este a székelyeknél

No. 5 from *10 könnyű zongoradarab*

Béla Bartók
(1881–1945)

Este a székelyeknél An Evening in the Village; **Könnyű zongoradarab** Easy Piano Pieces

From 1899 to 1903 the Hungarian composer Béla Bartók studied piano and composition at the Budapest Academy, where he later taught. In the first decade of the 20th century, he not only became a concert pianist but, alongside Kodály, began to collect Hungarian and, later, Romanian folksongs. This activity, together with the music of Debussy, exerted a profound influence on his style of composition. In addition, around the end of the First World War, he absorbed elements of the music of leading modernists Stravinsky and Schoenberg. In 1940, due to the rise of fascism and the outbreak of war in Europe, he emigrated to the USA, settling in New York, where he died shortly after the end of the war.

Bartók's *10 Easy Piano Pieces*, completed in Budapest in June 1908, was written for teaching purposes. Like so much of his music, in style it reflects the folk music of his native Hungary. No. 5, which has become very popular, was later orchestrated by the composer as the first of his *Hungarian Sketches* of 1931. The piece is given here in the composer's later, revised version. In the final section (bb. 45, 48 and 51) the melody notes are to be sustained by the pedal while the chords are struck.
Source: *Zehn leichte Klavierstücke/Tíz könnyű zongoradarab* (Budapest: Editio Musica, 1950)

18

Tempo primo

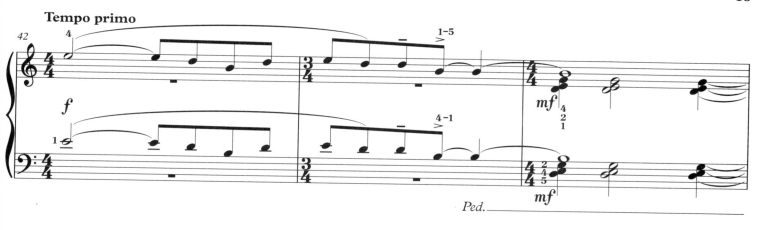

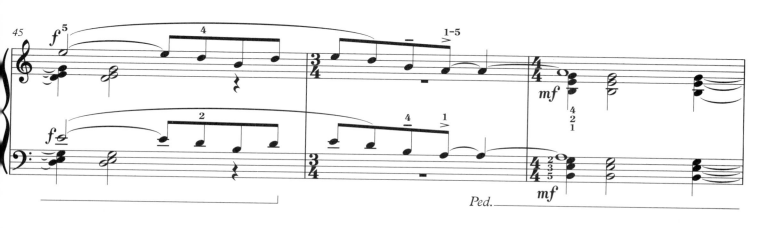

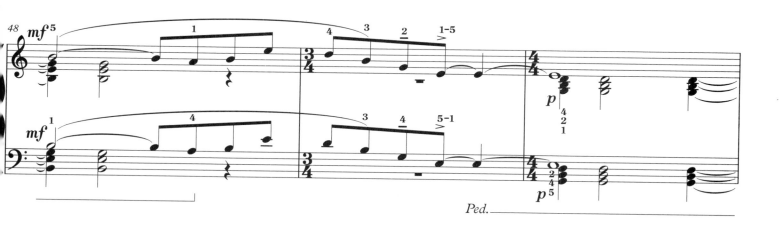

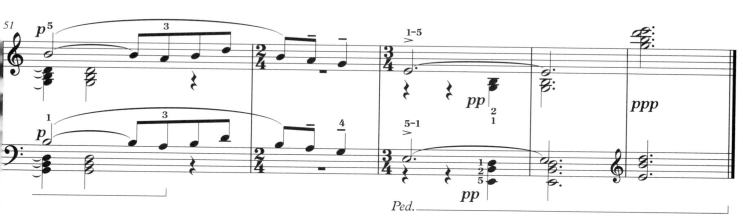

C:2

Cache-cache

No. 4 from *Pour les enfants*, Vol. 4

Alexandre Tansman
(1897–1986)

Cache-cache Hide-and-Seek; **Pour les enfants** For Children

The Polish-born composer and pianist Alexandre Tansman studied at the conservatory in his native town of Łódź, later furthering his studies in Warsaw. In 1919 he emigrated to France, settling in Paris, where he became acquainted with the music of Ravel, Stravinsky, Bartók and Prokofiev. From 1927 he toured internationally as a concert pianist and conductor. During the Second World War, he moved to the USA, living in Hollywood, where he was on friendly terms with Stravinsky. He returned to France in 1946.

The four volumes of Tansman's *Pour les enfants* contain in all 46 pieces of progressively increasing difficulty. Each piece has a programmatic title as a guide to the interpreter. 'Cache-cache' seems to evoke the sheer fun of the hide-and-seek game, while the offbeat accents capture the element of surprise.

Source: *Pour les enfants: quatre recueils de petites pièces pour piano*, Vol. 4 (Paris: Max Eschig, 1934)

60s Swing

No. 1 from *Swinging Rhythms*

C:3

Evelien Vis
(born 1956

Evelien Vis studied piano and singing at the Royal Conservatoire in The Hague. She sang in the Dutch and Flemish Broadcasting Choir for 17 years (1985–2002) and then became a secondary school music teacher in the Brussels area. She now works as a piano teacher, vocal coach (and accompanist) and composer. Her piano pieces, written for her students, often stem from improvisation and are swing or blues in style.

The composer has written that '60s Swing' is intended to be played with a jazzy feeling and to sound as if improvised. Bars 12–13, for example, are like an off-the-cuff retake on bb. 4–5. In the middle section (bb. 17–24), the 'improvisation' lies in the bass – here one can imagine the sound of a double bass or trombone. The last two bars of the piece are meant to sound like an echo.